Just Hold On:

*A Journey through Depression
with Faith and Hope*

Just Hold On:

*A Journey through Depression
with Faith and Hope*

Muffy Loiko

authorHOUSE®

AuthorHouse™
1663 Liberty Drive
Bloomington, IN 47403
www.authorhouse.com
Phone: 1-800-839-8640

First published by AuthorHouse   09/13/2011

ISBN: 978-1-4634-7460-7 (sc)
ISBN: 978-1-4567-9410-1 (ebk)

Printed in the United States of America

CONTENTS

Dedicated with loving thanks to Mom and Dad for showing me Faith.

Thank you Jeff and Gunner for giving me Hope.

My love to Jeff, Mom, Dad, Johnny, Linda, Alexis, Ab, Ed, Jamie, Jacob, Tony and Tressa and of course my heart . . . . Gunner <3

Introduction

The purpose of writing this book is to help others. There are so many people who suffer from anxiety and depression feel that they are alone. So many suffer in silence. I wanted to be a voice, a voice for the silent.

I am not a professional. My story is based on my personal experiences, my personal pain, and triumphs. My illness was not diagnosed until I was an adult. I always knew that I was different. My feelings were just not the same as others, and I never knew why. As I continue on my journey I have a better understanding of who I am and why.

It is my hope that if you see yourself or someone you know in these pages, you will share my story of hope and faith. There is help.

Please remember even in your deepest pain, to just hold on.

*Bill is a name change.

Chapter 1

Depression Does Not Discriminate

Maybe you know me? I could be your daughter, sister, auntie, wife, and or friend. I could even be your Momma. Sometimes you may not know me at all even though I look like someone you love. But, don't worry; it is okay, because sometimes I do not know myself. This is usually when my illness is not under control. I talk to God a lot, and I ask for help. Sometimes it is day to day. Sometimes it is minute by to minute. The illness I search to deal with and control is deep inside me, and it has a name:, it is depression.

I am not asking for you to understand it. My God, I live with it, and I do not understand it. I am asking of you, what I have to ask of myself on a regular basis: "Please be patient with me. Be kind and gentle." If you ask why, you will get the same answer I get: silence.

I am a thirty-eight-year-old wife and mother. I have everything I could ever ask for: a beautiful family, loving husband, nice home, amazing son, good friends, and a job that I love. So I ask myself, why am I depressed? I try not to be, but you know what? I just am. I cannot help it. I do not choose to have depression; I just do.

Weeks, even months, will go by, and I may even forget about my "condition." Then, all of a sudden, out of the blue, when I least expect it, depression reminds me. It reminds me it has control over me. I may yell or curl up in a ball, but mostly I cry. I cry long and hard. Do I feel better when I am done? No, I cry some more. Sometimes I can sleep; sometimes I cannot. Depression makes me so very tired. It is like a bad trick someone played on me. I ask for help, and no one responds. How can anyone help? Nobody has any idea how deep my pain is; it hurts. How long will this one last? Will it last a few hours? Days? I just don not know, so I pray some more.

Chapter 2

I Knew

Even as a small child, I had a sense of being different from everybody else. It was not the way I looked or the family I grew up in; it was something inside. I knew early on that somewhere in my heart was deep sadness. It was unexplainable and unclear; I just knew it was there. I did not feel other people had it.

Later in life, when I went to counseling, many tried to dig deep into my childhood. Something had to have gone wrong; there must be something hidden. I have to say, I had a great childhood. I had two wonderful parents who were sure to provide us with the best of everything, including love and discipline. My dad worked hard at the family business, and my mom was a stay-at-home mom. We had a clean house and warm brownies when we got off the school bus. I have two older brothers, an older sister, and a younger brother—plenty of people to protect and play with me. We had a cottage on the lake in the summer with boating, water skiing, and tubing; we had mini bikes; and we went on family outings. In the winter, we had snowmobiles to ride and were encouraged to get involved with many activities. So why am I so sad? What is wrong with me?

So many times I remember my dad saying, "What are you crying about?" I would reply, "I don't know." I really did not know, but that was not the answer my parents wanted to hear. I did hear, "She is so whiny," "She is so clingy," and "What's she crying about now?"

On Christmas and my birthday, I was especially emotional. These days were really built up in my mind, and neither event ever met my expectations. They would be such letdowns for me. Looking back, I see how hard my family worked at making my days special. It did not matter what they did or how wonderful these days were; I was sure to be disappointed.

I was different on the inside, and I knew it.

But I also knew about faith, faith in God. We would go to church every weekend and attend Sunday school. In the evening, all five children would kneel in front of the couch and say prayers. There would be some giggling, but later in life, this prayer time touched my heart.

Chapter 3

Growing Up

When I entered school, I easily made friends. Outwardly, I would usually smile, laugh, and be silly. I was a good student, and being accepted was important to me. I was a good athlete and always a team player. However, silently I would cry myself to sleep. I did not feel that anyone would understand, especially my parents. They worked hard to give me everything, so what in the world would I have to be sad about? My siblings were good to me. We had traditional sibling rivalries, but when I was teased or called a name, it seemed to hurt me more than others. Other people could get past it, move on, and laugh it off. For me, it hurt in my soul, and it hurt for a long, long time.

I remember hot sunny days at the lake; everyone would be swimming and playing outside. Mom would come in and see me curled in a blanket on the couch. She would say, "What are you doing in here on a beautiful day like this? Get outside." I wanted stay in, be by myself.

When my parents went away, it was excruciatingly hard for me. I took it so personally: *Why in the world would they want to leave me? Is it because I cry? Is it because I am whiny?* I knew it was entirely my fault that they left. I would sit by the window for hours. I would get myself so worked up that I would get hives. On many occasions, I would need to go to the hospital for my condition. Why couldn't I just get over it and deal? I could not talk to my parents on the phone; the sound of their voices completely broke my heart. I watched and listened to my siblings talk to them about their adventures; they were so happy hearing from them. Why could I not be like them?

I noticed. I noticed I was different. I also noticed I was not alone; I always had the presence of God with me.

Adolescence hit, and my inward struggles became visible. My emotions were all over the place. Of course, it was brushed off as typical. Teen girls go through different emotions and are changing and growing. I was not the typical teen girl. Every night when I would go to bed, I would get up and check to be sure the door was locked. I so feared someone would come in and hurt my family; it would keep me up at night. I would go down into the basement, which was a scary place for me when I was a young child; I was afraid my mom had forgotten to unplug the iron. I was convinced the house would burn down. My fears were not normal. Other people did not obsess about this stuff; I just knew it. I did not know how to control the anxiety I felt. So, I prayed. I prayed God would keep my family safe. I had such a deep fear something bad was going to happen. As I think about it now, I can still feel my heart pounding. I still sense the pain of something bad happening to my family.

I was also very clumsy. I was constantly hurting myself. I cannot count how many times I went to the emergency room. I had a stack of x-rays. At one point, I remember the doctor asking my mom questions. She replied, "I know what you are getting at, and no, I do not beat her." Little did anyone know that it was I who beat me. I was constantly beating myself up.

I was never good enough. I was never smart enough. I certainly was never pretty enough. I was a "big-boned" girl with no self-confidence. My outward silliness and laughter hid my inside pain.

I was a good athlete, not great, but I played and put in a lot of time. High school came, and I had many friends; school was good for me. The social environment was the best. But I wanted more. More what? Attention? I started drinking. Of course I was hiding it, just as I had been hiding my pain. I was stealing alcohol from my parents, drinking before school—anytime really. Maybe I was hoping I would get caught. Maybe I was doing it to get rid of my inside pain. I just know it continued all through high school.

I dated a couple of boys, but no one was really interested in the big-boned girl with curly hair. When I was a senior, I started dating a freshman. It felt great to have a boy pay attention to me, to want to be with me. I fell in love with him, but somewhere mixed inside with all my pain, I knew we where just too different. Our families, our upbringings, and our values were not the same. But it did not matter; somebody loved me!

I did not go away to college. I could not leave my home, my family, and my boyfriend. If I left, something bad would happen; I just knew it. I went to a local community college and worked part time with children as a preschool aide, and I went to all my high school boyfriend's activities. I discovered a great love for children. I wanted to be a teacher. That was something

I was good at; that was my gift. But I could not go away to college. I could not leave the people I loved; my heart would not let me. I continued to take classes and worked in preschool programs. Life was pretty good. I still lived at home with my parents and paid them minimal rent. I could not imagine leaving my parents' house. It was a safe place for me, a comfort zone; my daddy would be there to protect me. I had love, faith, family, friends, and a job that I liked. Finally I was okay.

Chapter 4

Striving To Be Happy

I was sitting up in my bedroom, and my boyfriend, Bill came up. He pulled out a small but very beautiful diamond and said, "Want to get married? I have to go; I have a softball game." Of course I said, "Yes!" We had been dating for three and a half years; was not marriage the next logical step in my life? Then he left and went to his softball game, which was the beginning of many signs that I was not his first priority. But it did not matter; I was getting married!

I went downstairs where my mother and sister were, and I actually hid my hand with the ring on it. I did not think they would be happy for me; there had been some rough spots in our relationship, but I pretended all was well. I did not have my parents' blessings right away. They asked me to live with him for a year; if after that time, I still wanted to marry him, I would have their blessings. I explained to them that that was not how I was raised. In God's eyes, you do not live together before you get married. Finally, they supported me; they just wanted me happy, and I was! Or so I thought.

Planning a wedding with my mom and my sister was great fun. My wedding day was a magical day. It was absolutely perfect. I had a big wedding in the church, music, bridesmaids, groomsmen, and a huge and beautiful reception. I had my parents' acceptance, and over three hundred people where there. I thought I looked beautiful. I was twenty-three, and my new husband was twenty. Oh, what a beautiful day.

We were renting a small house on a lake, and it was perfect. However, it did not take long to see small signs of our different upbringings come to light. He was young and wanted to be with his friends and play softball. I was constantly nagging about one subject or another; I would always find something. Three months into our marriage, I found out that God had blessed me with the greatest gift I will ever receive: I was pregnant.

When my doctor told me over the phone, I just cried. I was scared. I had one child in Bill; was I ready for another? My doctor told me to shower, take a deep breath, and go tell my family. I was going to need all the support I could get. I was going to be someone's mom. I was going to have a baby—someone who was going to be completely dependant on me!

I was still so dependent on my parents for love, support and guidance; I was so scared.

The preparation began for the new life I would bring into this world. After a couple of weeks, I was happy and ready to accept this new lifelong challenge. I had a great pregnancy, felt good, and worked right up to the delivery. I was induced for my delivery. My husband would keep looking up from his Sports Illustrated book, and I would get an occasional, "Relax." That was it, the extent of my support that day. I never wanted to hear the word *relax* ever again in my life. Then my miracle came to life: my son was born. The first thing I did was call my daddy.

Days in the hospital were filled with happiness and company. Bill was not there much; he had to work, and he had his softball games. On the last night of our stay, the hospital put on a couples dinner, by candlelight. I had placed the order and gotten all ready; dinner was at 6:00. I was so excited to spend an evening with my son's dad. At 6:30, he still had not shown up; he had a softball game. At 7:00, they took the candle and the dinner away. I have no idea what time he showed up. I just know my door was closed, my lights were off, and I was crying, hard. My beautiful boy and I were to go home the next day. We could leave around 11:00. I waited for Bill until 1:30; he could not get out of work. He quickly picked us up and dropped us off at my parents' instead of at our home; he did not have time for that.

Shortly after getting home and settled, we had to move. They were selling the house we were renting, and we did not have money to purchase it. We moved into a mobile home in a park. It was certainly not the life I was accustomed to, but it was the life I chose. I was going to make the best of it. It was our home. My sadness grew by the day. My nagging and yelling continued. Bill was gone more and more. This marriage was toxic for all of us. There were days when I felt out of control, and my choices were not the best. My life was crumbling. But I had my son, my unconditional strength.

By the time our son was two, we both knew the marriage was over. My pain was so deep that my mom took me to the doctor; I could not function on my own. Bill and I continued to both live in the trailer for a while and split the nights between us there. When it was my night to leave, I would meet Jeff, a man who worked for my dad. He was going through a divorce, and I liked his company; he was kind to me. It was a sad, hurtful, and horrible divorce. I moved into low-income housing. Bill stayed in the trailer park. I was solely responsible for our boy while he partied and went out.

My sadness was at the deepest level it had ever been. I had never in my life imagined that pain. I created it! I remember driving across the bridge and feeling my heart pound; I could not breathe. It was so intense, and I was so frightened. My child was in the backseat. I had to pull over as soon as I got off the bridge. I went right to my doctors, where they took me right in. I was convinced I was having a heart attack. I soon found out that that had been my first of many panic attacks due to my anxiety.

I tried hard to make my low-income apartment the "happy house." My boy and I played, read books, and laughed. On the outside, I wanted him to see a strong and happy mom! One the inside, I was dying. I was back to bad choices and decisions—anything to cause myself the pain that I deeply deserved. How could I have done this to myself?

I functioned for one reason only: I had a beautiful boy depending on me. I would not let him down . . . ever.

I was fortunate that my depression was not debilitating. I could still get out of bed every day. I could still do my job with a smile on my face. I could always take care of my son. He was and always will be my greatest gift from God.

But I had heard it all:

Pull yourself together.

Just snap out of it.

What do you have to be sad about?

There are people in this world worse off than you.

You should consider yourself lucky.

Stop feeling sorry for yourself.

Chapter 5

Finding Kindness

I began to spend more time with Jeff. I liked being around him, he drank with me, and he was fun. Rumors swirled about us. I did not care. He helped me forget my pain. He was one of the kindest people I had ever met. When I realized how much time we were spending together and how much he drank, I told him that he had to make a decision. I said, "If you choose to drink, I choose not to have you around my kid." I guess we mattered to him; he did not drink in front of my son again. In fact, after some of his own pain and growing up, he never drank again. It seemed as if my son and I were his life. When Jeff gave me a diamond, I could not accept it. I did not deserve happiness. He asked me to keep the ring, and I said, "No. I may never be ready to marry you, and I do not want that pressure." In the end, I kept the ring and wore it on my right hand, never intending to move it to my left hand. If I ever felt that I was worthy of marrying him, I would want a new ring; a fresh start.

I watched Jeff around my son, how kind and patient he was. He was such a strong, positive role model in my son's life at the time, and my son did not have other strong role models like him. I loved watching their interactions; it made me happy. He made me happy. He cooked us dinner, took us to the beach, and did fun stuff with us! But at night, when Jeff went home and I was alone with my boy, I felt something was missing. It was not pain I felt; it was deep, deep sadness and loneliness. After my son would fall asleep, I would cry until there were no tears left. I prayed, I held on, and I had hope that tomorrow would always be a new day.

I began looking a Jeff differently. I always thought he was handsome. Now I was feeling something else. I knew that I was falling in love. It was different from how I had ever felt before. I had so much respect for him and his gentle kindness. He was so good to us. I never nagged, yelled, or barked at him. My son and I came first to him. I did not deserve this person in my life. But my son did. Jeff was one of the most incredible men I had ever met. I felt safe with him, something I had not felt in so many years.

Driving down the road one day with Jeff and my son, I simply said, "I am ready." He pulled over and said, "What?" I replied, "I am ready to marry you." He pulled over and cheered, and my son cheered, too. I cried, but for a change these were happy tears. We eloped shortly after with family. My parents threw us a beautiful outdoor reception. We started building our own home, figuratively and literally.

Our new life was beginning. It was a wonderful world. I had hot coffee on my bureau every morning, and I saw kindness I had never known. Jeff told me every single day that I was beautiful. He thanked me for being in his life and sharing my son. It was so hard for me to hear his kind words, so hard for me to accept them. For once, I gave goodness and kindness in return. Many people told me he was too good to be true. I was constantly waiting for the other shoe to drop. He was so good, and he was true He loved my son and I unconditionally. There were times when he saw glimpses of my depression. He never judged me, he held me during my storms, and he was my rock.

We attended church as a family even though he was not Catholic. I felt safe. I was certain God brought this man into my life to save us. I was grateful for that. I never once took his love for granted. It was a deep and caring love that every person should have in her lifetime. I had a beautiful family. I wanted more.

Chapter 6

Pain

We struggled with infertility, which deepened my depression. I was not worthy. I did not deserve another child. The doctor visits, the tests, the pain, and the medication all played havoc on my already unstable emotions. I was losing control.

Thank God Jeff did not give up on me or us! After five years of riding on the emotional roller coaster, I realized I could not do it any more. We stopped trying to have another child. Now I had to get my life back, my emotions in check. I had to take a deep breath and just hold on.

I began once again to focus on what we had, all of the positive things in our life. It brought me back to peace, happiness, and an appreciation of what we were. I continued to watch Jeff be the best father any one could ask for. Our family relationships grew and deepened.

We were involved with our son's school, athletics, and traveling. Jeff was on the board of directors for many events. He was still working for my dad. We had a good life. I still had periods in my life where I was so sad that I would just cry for a long time. My son would say, "Mom is just taking a nap again." It was in middle school when he became very aware of my sadness.

He was in seventh grade when I felt myself spiraling. I was constantly on edge for no reason. I would binge and feel guilty, and then I would vomit. I would cry. I looked in the mirror, and I did not recognize the woman looking back at me. She was completely helpless. I had to do something. I called the doctor in a frantic, desperate state. My emotions had been out of control for days. The tears would not stop. It was affecting my son. I saw it in his eyes. I was not okay anymore; I could not do this on my own. I was so very scared. I needed help. It was then, after many discussions and a round of counseling, when I was diagnosed with depression and anxiety. I went on Prozac. I had heard terrible rumors about the medication, but I had to try something. It took weeks to regulate my medications.

I have a label: I have a mental illness. I have depression and anxiety. Now how can I make my family, my friends, and myself understand that it is not anyone's fault? It is who I am. It is who I have always been, but finally I realized I needed help.

Chapter 7

Trying

In the meantime I began to feel better. We continued with church, and my husband had become Catholic. We would pray and talk. I had hope. My son would spend a lot of time in our computer room. I do not know if he understood what was going on with me. I always tried to be open and honest with him, sometime maybe too much so. I found a book that talked about mental illness, and I just left it by his computer. I needed him to know none of this was his fault. If anything, he was the one who saved my life.

I remember people talking about suicide, and I remember saying I could never imagine doing that. I could. I had imagined doing that. I had had a plan. Now I was getting help that I desperately needed. Thank God. I had done it; I had held on. I did a lot of reading about my illness. I worked hard at making my life better for everyone around me. I began journaling and focusing on the good things. I would write in my journal every day. I would write three things I was thankful for and note one kind thing I did to make a difference in someone else's life or offer a prayer to someone in need. Focusing on the good helped me not to focus on my depression.

There are times when I do not even see it coming. I think I am fine when I wake up in the morning. Then *bam!* All of a sudden, there is my friend depression. I call it my friend because it is part of my life, and we have to learn to get along and manage. I am tired, I am angry, and I wish I could just crawl into my bed. I want to be alone. I want to cry alone. Days like those are a lot of work. I have a job to do. I have people that depend on me.

I pray. I take a deep breath and another and another. I keep breathing.

Chapter 8

I Can Do This

Today I woke up and felt very tired. I knew I just was not myself. I had to go to work and put on my happy face. I had to do my best acting job, teaching. I had to engage my students and help them learn and believe they are working on being the best they can be. I can do it; I have done it many times before. It is a busy day for me: work, church with my daddy (which I love), and my niece's dance recital. All of these things are good things, but I am not good at not having enough time. Transition time is very important to me. On top of all of this, I am coming down with a cold. These are all minor things to most people, but they are not minor at all to me.

I know I am struggling. After work I try to get in a thirty-minute rest. I had just a brief time to close my eyes and regroup. It just seemed to make me more tired.

Then church ran late; they had a beautiful baptism, and I saw the beauty in the moment. But when I realized how rushed I was, I just stood and cried, and I was a half hour late for the recital.

I wanted a nice warm shower. I looked for something in the shower that I could cut with. There was nothing within reach, and part of me was thankful. Another part of me was sad; it would have been a way to take away my stress and pain. I did not search out something to hurt myself with. Instead I took my medication and went to bed.

Tomorrow would be a new day. Even if it was not sunny and warm, I believed. I believed I had just made it though a long, hard, and stressful day. There would be more. But I was okay. I did not hurt myself. I had a very good night's sleep. I had held on once again.

Some days are just easier than others. I know that rest and exercise are important to me, and if I do not get either, that will affect me. I need to take care of myself even on busy days. I will get through them. I will have hope.

Chapter 9

Remembering

I had another visitor enter my life. It was called fear. I had a very anxious and depressing few months, and it was time to try a new medication. I have fear that it would not work. I feared I would lose my family. Every time fear visits, I take a deep breath and remember I have to try.

I was reading a part of my journal, and I saw yet another piece of my illness. The tears streamed down my face as I read my entry. "It is strange for me; I feel like I am losing someone that saved my life. Today was my last day on Prozac; I have been weaning off it, and today was my last one. I am transitioning to a new medication. It has to work. Thank you, Prozac, for saving my life."

My adult life continued with doctors and changes in medications. I was managing my mental illness. I was good at my teaching job. No one ever had any idea about my pain and sadness. At that point, I was a master at covering it up. But whenever I looked in the mirror, I never liked what I saw. I never thought of myself as pretty (except on my wedding day) or good enough. So, I worked on being kind and looking happy. Every day my husband would tell me how beautiful I was, but they were just kind, empty words to me. I wonder if I will ever get to the point of accepting myself.

Over the years, I did counseling here and there. I have gone through many medication changes and many sleepless nights. My bouts of anxiety and depression have been somewhat under control, but they are never gone. I feel like there is always a shadow behind me, just waiting to catch up with me. And when it does, I am in big trouble. It never goes away. Sometimes it sleeps inside me for a very long time. I almost forget that it is there. Then it wakes up and reminds me that it can control me.

I know I have amazing support. I have been much more open and honest about my illness. I am stronger now, and I have more skills, but I am still scared. That shadow is always lurking, it again reminds me of the control it has. I know when the demons appear to just hold on, work through it with faith, and never give up hope.

Then when I least expect it, I have another rough spot in my life with this battle of depression. Every minor routine thing is a battle. It takes so much energy not to let myself just explode. I say a lot of prayers. My depression and anxiety affect my son and my husband more than anyone, and that makes me so sad. They are my "safe" people. I cry, I scream, and I say what hurts.

Oh, others do not understand the struggle. But how can they? I do not understand this. This time writing is actually calming for me. I feel myself settling for the first time in days. Does something set me off, or is it just the imbalance? I need to ask more questions. I am tired. I am sad.

But you would never know that about me.It is hard to hide my pain. If you see me, my mask is on. When I am alone, sometimes I just cry, and that is okay. One day at a time. Maybe tomorrow I will feel better. God will get me through this. I need to go remind my son and husband how much I love them.

Chapter 10

Hurting Me

The last few days have been very dreary and rainy. These days are hard for me. I love the sun. I love the way my body feels when it is warm, refreshed, and nourished. I know the weather can affect my depression, so I take extra care to be aware of the way I am feeling.

I went for a long walk. It was cool and drizzly, but it felt good to get out. When I went in to shower, I felt a little agitated and edgy—jumpy almost. My legs started itching. The warm water felt good on them, but I started to scratch. Yes, I scratched until it hurt. I got out of the shower, dried off, put lotion on, and got dressed. I put on shorts, just hoping the weather would warm up, and I put on a big, bulky sweatshirt. I was better. Then, as I was driving down the road, I looked down. There were bruised lines and scratches on my legs. It was no surprise; I had done this to myself before. It saddens me that I can continue to hurt myself; what saddens me more is that now it does not seem to bother me when people notice.

I think it is because I feel like I made it through. I will get better. This is just a bump in the road. I think about the next time I will feel that way and ask myself what changes I will make. Could I resist the scratching? Could I just rub lotion on my legs when I want to scratch? Could I go make a phone call? I am beginning to make plans now for the "what ifs." It is an action plan for struggling moments. Now I am impressed that I have jumped this hurdle. I learned another skill to help me with this disease.

Chapter 11

Deep Sadness

I often wonder what I did in this lifetime to deserve Jeff. He is my rock, my safe place. He has seen me at my worst, and he still stays with me. When I am not in a full-blown depressive state, just talking to him or listening to him will calm me. When I am in the midst of my deepest pain, he knows instinctively what I need. I know God sent him to me to take care of my son and me. I am grateful for him every single day. Every person deserves someone like Jeff. It saddens me that he has to live with my illness. It belongs as much to him as it does me. When I hurt, he hurts. He has taken me to the doctor, and he has stayed up with me at night. He has bandaged my wounds.

I do not remember the first time I cut myself. I do remember I was in deep, incredible, and agonizing pain.

Cutting does not necessarily mean going and getting a knife and slicing. It means getting anything in your reach to hurt yourself so you cannot feel the pain in your soul any more. I think the first time I cut myself was with a screw; I just kept scraping my arm over and over again. I felt pain; I saw blood. After instances like this, my rage would be over, but I would still be sad and have to take care of my wound. Then I would sleep for a long time. My body would finally be able to quiet. I had held on and made it through.

After that first time, I vowed I would never do that again. I knew it was extreme. But when the next round of my demons appeared, I forgot the promise I had made to myself. Before I knew it, I had scars up and down my arms. People would ask me what the marks were from. Of course, I would lie. I burned my arm in the oven. I scraped it. I just had to remember which lie I had told at any time. In the winter, it was easy; my arms were covered. But in the summer, I could not only feel my pain; I could see it.

Then I thought I was being clever. I would cut where no one would see, such as my hip or side. But I still knew it was wrong. If Jeff were around, he would stay with me. He would be sure I did not hurt myself. He would help me through my pain. I never knew what set me off, but all of a sudden I found myself in the middle of a very sad night. I was in a desperate state, deep in a rage. I went into the bathroom and saw a pair of scissors. I cut hard and deep. I saw flesh. This is the first time I had ever been scared. When I came out and Jeff saw what I had done, he said he had to take me to the hospital. I needed stitches. I could not go. I would have to tell them what I did. I was convinced they would admit me. Normal people do not harm themselves. I just cried.

I saw the sadness in Jeff's eyes. He was scared too. He got me tape and bandages, and we cried. We cried long and hard until we both fell asleep. I know God was watching over me that night. I woke up the next morning, with hope.

Please remember that I do not choose this disease. If I could make myself be in constant control, I would. I take my medication; I take the help and support. I go to the doctor. I still have that pain, though. My insides ache; I hurt so badly.

If I had another disease that was visible on the outside, would people be more tolerant and patient? I know that I am sick, and I work every day of my life to get better. I pray. Sometimes I pray, "God, help me." Sometimes I pray, "God, thank you for this great day." I say I am sorry to Jeff. I tell him I am sorry he has to live through this with me. But he does. God helps us, and we have an amazing life together. For that I am grateful.

If you see my scars, please know I am completely embarrassed. It is harm that I have caused myself. They are scars from the wounds I put on my own body in the midst of being in deep and utter sadness. Jeff gently says not to worry about the scars; it is all part of seeing healing.

Chapter 12

Sensitive

Wow. Sometimes my feelings can be really hurt. Even though I am almost fifty years old, other people's comments still affect my emotional well-being. I have never had good self-esteem, but as I get older I think somehow I am able to protect myself from unkind words. I have also stood up for myself when someone was cruel and said, "Why would you say that to me?"

When I am not in a very good space, words and actions still hit me hard. Little things really hurt, such as when people say, "Maybe you should lose a few pounds" or "You cannot do that job" or when someone gets invited to see a family member's new home and I do not. Even though I know I will eventually be invited, pain just has a way of creeping deep into my soul. This is part of my not being like everyone else. Why do I care what people do and say? Why does it matter? The answer is that that is who I am.

Outside factors definitely affect my inside soul. The external factors that I struggle with are what I am working on handing over to God. If it is not in my control, there is nothing I can do about it. I need to trust in God's plan for me.

I am trying to watch negative thoughts come into my head and let them pass right through. There is not room for them there. So I breathe. I know deep in my heart that every day will not feel like this. I will not be this sensitive or emotional every single day. Things do get better.

I remind myself of my amazing life, faith, family, home, and job. I see so many blessings all around me every single day. Sometimes I write them down to focus on the good. Sometime I just close my eyes. Sometimes I take my dog for a walk and listen for the children's laughter throughout our neighborhood.

I am always aware of my feelings and my emotions, good or bad.

I feel like I am constantly keeping myself in check. Tomorrow will be a better day.

Chapter 13

Time for Change

I am about to turn fifty my depression had taken me to the next level. I knew I had to make some serious changes. What I was doing was not enough. First I would try a medication change. Maybe mine was not working for me anymore. I knew more changes had to be made. I began to exercise more. I stepped out of my comfort zone of taking walks and began Zumba. I liked it. I liked the energy in the room. In just a couple of weeks, I felt comfortable. I also started yoga. I knew I had to learn how to calm my mind. It was very difficult for me, and I had trouble settling in, but I stuck with it. The next change I made was finding an acupuncturist. I found one who believed in Chinese medicine and natural healing. I was not willing to give up my medication, nor did he ask me to. But after a couple of sessions, it also seemed to be helping. I also got a dog, a beautiful yellow lab. I no longer had to wait for my son to visit to bring his dog. Every day when I came home, he was happy to see me. He needed exercise, so I would take him for a walk. We would play, and I would laugh. He was a good addition to my life.

I began to find myself at a quiet place. There was no chaos. I would pray and talk to God. I would thank Him for my good days. I would breathe more. I know that there is help out there; I just have to reach out and take it. I am thankful for the people in my life who love me unconditionally. Please do not tell me I will be all right; somewhere deep down I know that. Maybe just pray for me to hold on, keep my faith, and have hope.

In my late forties, I began reconnecting with my high school friends. Of course, they all knew how much I drank back in the day. Now they were my safe group, my old friends who loved me no matter what. I remember telling them about all my struggles. I told them about my cutting and my scars. I told them the truth, no lies. They did not judge me. They just cared.

It is important for me to surround myself with positive people. I try to be upbeat, avoid negativity, and do something good for another person every day.

My heart might hurt some days, but it is a good heart. It is strong and full of love. I have to remember that love does conquer all. If there is love, faith, and hope, I can beat this battle of mine, this battle with depression. I am going to keep fighting, keep working, keep improving, and keep finding new ways to live with this disease.

I am going to hang on.

Some Positive Reminders
If You Suffer from Depression

Have something higher than yourself to believe in. Have faith.

It is okay if your family does not understand. Provide them with knowledge and information.

Be gentle and kind to yourself every day.

Surround yourself with good people.

Have hope.

Avoid negative people.

Find something good in every day.

Write in a gratitude journal.

Do one kind thing for someone every single day, and write it in your journal to remind yourself of your own goodness.

Do not be afraid to ask for help.

Avoid negative self-talk.

Have a backup plan to substitute for negative behaviors.

Have positive affirmations posted where you can see them.

When someone says something kind to you, say thank you.

Find support from the National Alliance on Mental Illness (NAMI), family, and friends.

In the silence of a suffering heart, strength is born.

There will be moments when the one you counted on walks away; God will still be there.

Practice acceptance and patience.

Many things are possible for the person who has hope, and even more is possible for the person with faith.

Give the world the best you have.

He has a purpose for our every pain.

It is important for those of us who are hurting to know that our story is not finished.

Hope is knowing that pain is not permanent.